Just like the river, this colourful guide meanders through the breath-taking landscape of the Fowey Estuary and shares the history of its people and places in a bite-sized style.

G000096102

The unique and inspiring landscape of the River Fowey was formed 12,000 years ago, at the end of the last Ice Age.

For centuries Fowey and Polruan have been significant locations in the maritime story of Cornwall. The sailors and shipbuilders of the area have also made considerable contributions to Great Britain's naval and nautical achievements.

In Medieval times Fowey Harbour was the main port for Cornwall and as the mining industry boomed, Cornish tin, copper and china clay was shipped from Fowey to destinations all over the world.

From its source on Bodmin Moor to where the river meets the sea, the trade that has flowed along the Fowey river has provided jobs for thousands of local people and created significant wealth for many merchants, mariners, miners and landowners.

Once home to the Duchy of Cornwall and ancient Cornish kings, the banks of the River Fowey have been far from calm.

Bridges have been fought over during the Civil War, invasions have come from the French and in recent times, Fowey was a training base for the US Navy before they departed for the D-Day landings.

During peacetime, the Fowey Estuary has provided creative inspiration for numerous artists and writers. Today mariners and water lovers, walkers and tourists enjoy the many natural and historical riches, this fabulous part of Cornwall has to offer.

Like the ebb and flow of Fowey, this little reader will take you into creeks and coves and land you at ports, harbours and waterside villages. As you turn each page it is our hope that this book reveals the breadth and depth of wonder that the Fowey river has shaped and caressed for centuries.

This book celebrates the achievements of Fowey Harbour Commissioners whose guardianship has protected this precious place for the last 150 years and for future generations to come.

FOWEY HARBOUR

The River Fowey flows for 40kms.

The Fowey Estuary is a drowned ria valley fed by the Fowey and other tributaries including the Lerryn, Penpol and Pont rivers.

As the Fowey river broadens and shallows at Golant, it widens to over 0.5km. Its deepest point is between Bodinnick and Caffa Mill.

Faw-y or *Fawi* is the Cornish word for the Fowey river, which means "river of beech trees".

The headwaters of the Fowey rise 298 metres above sea level, at Fowey Well on Bodmin Moor.

The Fowey river catchment is the largest river basin in South Cornwall. It drains an area of 177 km² of central and southern Bodmin Moor providing Cornwall with 65% of its water supply.

Fenten Fawi (Cornish for Fowey Well) can be found approximately 1.6km northwest of Brown Willy, the highest point in Cornwall.

The granite uplands of Bodmin Moor were originally called Fowey Moor after the river they fed. The name was changed in the early 1800s when the Ordnance Survey renamed it in their first maps of the area.

The Fowey river flows through two Sites of Special Scientific Interest, a National Nature Reserve, and much of the estuary's 1,000 acres are designated as an Area of Outstanding Natural Beauty.

The Fowey river meets the English Channel at Punches Cross in Polruan to the east and St Catherine's Castle in Fowey, to the west.

Whilst the lower part of the harbour is deep enough to anchor some of the world's most luxurious cruise liners, the upper reaches of the estuary dry out at low tide.

As the river flows from the Cornish uplands to the English Channel, over 430 million litres of water flow through Fowey Harbour each day.

As the Fowey river leaves Bodmin Moor, it runs through Draynes Valley, an ancient oak woodland and Site of Special Scientific Interest.

Here the river flows through Golitha Falls, a National Nature Reserve.

The word "golitha" comes from the Cornish word for obstruction.

At Golitha Falls the Fowey river descends 90 metres creating spectacular cascades and waterfalls.

The ancient forest, gigantic boulders and steep-sided gorge make this a dramatic place to visit at any time of year. Take particular care if you are visiting after heavy rainfall.

After Golitha Falls, the Fowey river flows through the Glynn Valley and on into the magnificent grounds and estate of Lanhydrock.

Named after the Cornish word *res* meaning ford, Respryn has had a river crossing for over 700 years.

The five-arched bridge, which is about 40 metres long and 3 metres wide, dates back to medieval times. Once part of the old cart track from Bodmin to Looe, the bridge at Respryn was a significant strategic crossing in the navigation of inland Cornwall.

The bridge, which was constructed from granite and stone, has piers on either side with sharp cutwaters. Above there are corresponding refuges for pedestrians to step into, out of the narrow road.

Respryn Bridge played an important role during the English Civil War. During 1644, it was at the heart of the conflict between the Royalists led by Sir Richard Grenville and the Parliamentarians and the Earl of Essex. The Royalists secured the crossing and, to celebrate the victory, Sir Richard Robartes planted the avenue of trees that lead up to Lanhydrock House today.

Set in over 1,000 acres of parkland, woodland and enchanting riverside paths, Lanhydrock House is one of the National Trust's most visited properties.

Up until the mid 1500s, the Lanhydrock estate was owned by the Augustinian Priory of St Petroc in Bodmin. It was purchased in 1620 by Sir Richard Robartes, and shortly afterwards the construction of Lanhydrock House began.

The house, which has 49 rooms, was built out of granite and originally designed with four sides, shaped around a central courtyard. In April 1881, most of the house was destroyed by an enormous fire, which damaged everything except the Gatehouse and North Wing. Only a U shape remains today.

As well as a magnificent house, Lanhydrock is home to 22 acres of garden and over 120 different species of cream and white magnolias. In the spring, these majestic trees offer up their pastel flowers and the woodland floor becomes a carpet of bluebells not to be missed.

After Lanhydrock, the Fowey continues south towards Lostwithiel and passes the ancient walls of 13th century Restormel Castle.

Restormel Castle, originally built by the Normans, was gifted to Edward of Woodstock, the Black Prince, in 1337 as he was granted the brand new title of Duke of Cornwall.

The walls of what would have been a top-notch Cornish residence are over 2.4 metres thick and at full height they stand over 7.6 metres above ground. The castle is 38 metres in diameter and is surrounded by a 15 x 4 metre ditch.

Today the outstanding remains of this circular shell keep are protected by English Heritage. Only 71 examples of this type of fortification remain across England and Wales and Restormel Castle is the most intact.

11kms upstream from the river mouth, Lostwithiel Bridge marks the upper limit of the Fowey's tidal navigation. From here to the river mouth the Fowey and its shoreline are protected by Fowey Harbour Commissioners.

The original bridge, which was built by the Normans who founded Lostwithiel, was first documented in 1280 and had nine arches. The foundations of the four westerly ones are believed to be under North Street.

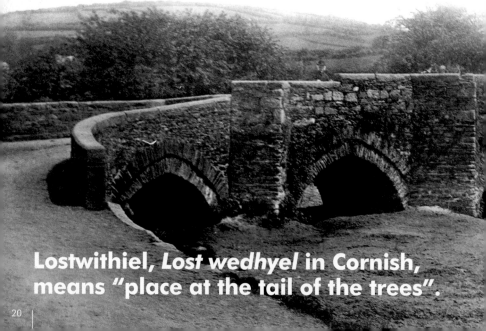

Lostwithiel, *Lost wedhyel* in Cornish, means "place at the tail of the trees".

The crossing was rebuilt during the 15th century and, during the English Civil War, it narrowly escaped being blown up by the Parliamentarian Army.

During the 18th century, four easterly arches were added and, until the A390 bypass was built in 1939, Lostwithiel Bridge was the main road between Liskeard and St Austell.

One of the most momentous occasions for Lostwithiel's ancient bridge was on Wednesday 17th November 2010 when the BBC national news broadcast live from the river.

After a night of torrential rain and gale-force winds the bridge was closed and many of its arches were blocked by branches and debris.

Locals feared that the 700-year-old structure would collapse under the force of the water. Cars parked along Quay Street were swept over 50 metres and further along the road, floodwater was waist deep. Many residents had to be evacuated from their riverside homes by the local fire brigade and Royal National Lifeboat Institution (RNLI).

For just a moment, Lostwithiel Bridge was the most famous bridge in Britain, seen by millions of BBC viewers worldwide. Its ancient structure withstood the flood and, within days, the water level had returned to normal.

During the 12th and 13th centuries, Lostwithiel was the administrative capital of Cornwall, seat of the Duke of Cornwall and a thriving Stannary town.

The Great Hall, known as the Duchy Palace today, was at the heart of East Cornwall's tin trade. Constructed by the Earl of Cornwall during the late 13th century, the Stannary Palace as it was originally entitled was built as a court and coinage hall, where tax officials weighed, valued and stamped tin.

The surviving building, which was designed to replicate Westminster, can be found on the corner of Fore Street and Quay Street and is believed to be the oldest non-ecclesiastical building in Cornwall.

Lostwithiel was once known as "The Port of Fawi".

During the 14th century Lostwithiel was the second busiest port on the south coast of England.

The depth of the river in the upper reaches of the estuary enabled seafaring ships to dock at what is now Coulson Park and load precious tin.

By the end of the century sediment from excessive tin streaming upstream on the moor had travelled down and silted up the riverbed. Only boats with a shallow draft could dock. Lostwithiel's shipping trade was lost to Fowey but the harbour wall on the walk towards Shirehall Moor serves as a reminder of this once thriving port.

During the 19th century, Lostwithiel boomed off the back of mining iron ore. The ore was mined from Restormel Royal Mine 1km northwest of Lostwithiel in the Lanivet area. It was carried by horse-drawn wagons through the town to the jetty, where it was shipped down-river in barges.

The iron industry ended at the turn of the 20th century and the river was used to barge limestone to the limekilns on Quay Street, to be turned into fertilizer.

Brunel's Great Western Railway arrived in Lostwithiel in 1859. The maintenance works (now Brunel Quays), provided employment for over a century.

In 1932, as the need for railway workers diminished, a milk factory, known as The Creamery, was developed and became the town's major employer until 1991.

Today Lostwithiel is regarded as the "Antiques Capital of Cornwall" and many of the town's events take place along the river. Lostfest, Ginfest and Sing Along the River bring the waterside Parade Gardens to life with music, brass bands and local food and drink.

If you want a glimpse of Lostwithiel's maritime heritage, wander downstream and let the banks of the Fowey lead you through Coulson Park, along the quay and then on to Shirehall Moor.

Coulson Park, which opened in 1907, was named after Nathaniel Coulson, a San Francisco property magnate who was raised in Lostwithiel after being abandoned by his father.

As the Fowey river meanders beyond Lostwithiel, the valley floor opens out to reveal the salt marshes of Shirehall Moor.

The intertidal salt marsh of Shirehall Moor has been a designated nature reserve since 2007.

The 23-acre reserve, which was once the local refuse site, is now home to a wide range of birdlife including mute swans, mallards, grey herons, little egrets and kingfishers.

Salt marshes are an important habitat and biodiversity hot spot that link the land and the sea. Very often these special areas also provide natural sea defences acting as floodplains in times of high rainfall and spring tides.

The abundant sections of reed beds and bulrushes that populate this section of the Fowey estuary provide refuge and food for water voles, rodents and a wide variety of small and wading birds.

The Lostwithiel U3A group (University of the 3rd Age), hold regular bird watching walks along Shirehall Moor and have spotted bar-tailed godwits, blue, coal and long-tailed tits, curlews, Canada geese, oystercatchers, redshanks, sand martins, dunlins and peregrine falcons.

In order to survive, a kingfisher needs to eat its bodyweight in fish every single day.

If you are lucky enough to catch a glimpse as they dart past your eyes, you'll notice how outstanding and vibrant their bluey-green and orange feathers are against their habitat.

Expert fishermen, kingfishers enjoy a diet of small fish, shrimps and tadpoles. They tend to inhabit clean, shallow, slow-moving rivers with a plentiful supply of small fish.

Kingfishers love the wooded banks of the Fowey because the overhanging trees provide excellent perches to overlook their prey swimming beneath.

Instead of building a nest kingfishers make a burrow and prefer to breed in areas where the riverbank is slightly soft. The tunnels to their burrows can be up to 140cms long and take weeks to create.

Kingfishers breed between March and April, laying up to seven eggs, which hatch between 16 and 21 days later. They can have several broods per season and their young are ready to leave the burrow at less than four weeks old.

The church of St Winnow, which was recorded in the Domesday book, was featured in the 1970s series of *Poldark* and in the Sky TV drama *Delicious*.

The 15th century church is believed to stand on the site of a 7th century oratory dedicated to Saint Winnoc. The modest church dominates this tiny hamlet, which has a profound sense of tranquillity and timelessness about it.

Angela du Maurier, Daphne du Maurier's sister, is buried in the graveyard and just opposite is the resting place of the Vivian family, once the Barons of Cornwall.

Inside the church, the wooden carvings on the bench ends are believed to date back to the 15th century and are some of the finest examples in Cornwall.

St Winnow has a tiny population and just ten or so houses. The local farm runs a small campsite and has a fascinating free museum exhibiting old farm machinery and tools. During the summer season, Angie's caravan café, which serves hot drinks and cream teas, is a great stop off for walkers strolling between Lostwithiel and Lerryn.

One of the largest marine residents of the Fowey Estuary is known locally as Serena, a common seal.

If you're on a canoeing or kayaking trip in the upper reaches of the river, keep your eyes peeled. She's most often spotted hauled out and snoozing along the bank.

Common seals, also known as harbour seals, prefer the sheltered shores of estuaries and sandbanks where they can haul out and have a nap or give birth.

Common seals enjoy a diet of fish but will also eat squid, whelks, crabs and mussels.

Less common than grey seals, who are the most regular visitors to the Cornish coast, common seals used to be hunted for their skins. This has had an enormous impact on their numbers. Today, the species is protected in Britain under the 1970 Conservation of Seals Act.

The ancient waterside woodland of the Ethy estate is believed to have been the inspiration for the *Wild Wood* in Kenneth Grahame's books *Wind in the Willows*.

Ethy Woods extend from the village of Lerryn to Ethy Rock. They are home to some of Cornwall's oldest oak trees and particularly rare lichen *Arthonia ilicinella*.

The famous Ethy Hoard was discovered in Ethy Woods in June 2000 by two metal detectorists from St Austell.

After detecting a single Roman coin in a small pottery jar along the edge of an ancient cart track, stronger detector readings led them to a moss-covered mound pushed against a bank of bedrock. After removing the earth, they found the remains of pottery vessels jammed with over 500 Roman coins.

After thorough investigations of the area by the Royal Cornwall Museum, the Ethy Hoard as it became known was listed as a treasure trove of over 1095 silver radiates, which date back to the 3rd century.

The Ethy Hoard was moved to the Royal Cornwall Museum, Truro, in 2001. Despite the large number of coins and their age, an inquest at Bodmin Magistrates Court declared the find to be worth just £4,000.

The River Lerryn is the largest tributary to the Fowey.

The village, which is named after the Lerryn river, is situated at the lowest crossing point.

When the tide flows out, it reveals an enchanting series of stepping stones, that make it possible to cross the river on foot. The single-lane bridge carries vehicular traffic.

Lerryn Bridge was built in 1572 but a crossing has been recorded there since 1289. While the bridge was being strengthened during the 1980s, engineers discovered the original granite carriageway lying beneath the road.

On the southern bank of the river lie the remains of a private park known as Tivoli Gardens.

The pleasure gardens and recreational park were created by Frank Parkyn who made his money from china clay mining. Parkyn bought the woodland from the Rashleigh Estate in 1911 and construction of the gardens began during 1920.

The grounds, which featured a pond, fountains, a plunge pool, pavilion, sports field and bandstand, were named Tivoli Gardens after a park in Copenhagen, which Parkyn had visited. The area is completely overgrown now but some of the structures still remain.

The first printed record of the Lerryn Regatta was its mention in the 1870 edition of the Royal Cornwall Gazette.

Organised by the Parkyn family of Mixton House, historians believe Lerryn Regatta was an annual event until the outbreak of the First World War. After the war, it was revived at Tivoli Park where it remained until the 1960s.

Frank Parkyn died in 1940 but a small group of local volunteers kept the event going, which included a field sports competition and swimming and rowing races.

The highlight of the programme was a torchlight parade through the village and a dance with live music. At its peak organisers believe over 5,000 visitors attended.

Regatta events ceased during the Second World War but it was revived once more for the Royal Coronation of Elizabeth II in 1953 and the last regatta took place in 1968.

Today, Lerryn's festival spirit lives on in the annual Seagull race held during the Christmas Holidays. It's a fancy dress event and competitors can race anything on the river, as along as its propelled by a Seagull outboard motor.

The Red Store in Lerryn was built in 1840 as an office for a local agricultural merchant. It was used as a store during the Second World War and today it is looked after by the parish council and provides exhibition space for local artists and craftspeople.

"Lerryn river" in Cornwall is *Dowr Leryon*, which means "river of floods", and the translation could not be more appropriate. Most locals know that Lerryn car park and the road that runs alongside the river flood regularly on a spring tide. Visitors, however, get quite a surprise when they return from a walk or a meal at the Ship Inn to find their car by surrounded water.

The Lostwithiel and Fowey Railway line opened in 1869.

The purpose of the rail link was to transport china clay from the mines in the St Austell area to Fowey Docks. A passenger service ran from 1876 until 1965.

The picturesque route, which runs almost entirely along the Fowey estuary from Lostwithiel to Caffa Mill has been a favourite overnight stopping point for the Royal Train.

In 2004 The Sun newspaper published a photograph of Oasis star Noel Gallagher walking along the line, while he was recording an album at Sawmills near Golant. Gallagher was questioned by the British Transport Police and reminded that he was actually trespassing, which was a crime.

From Lostwithiel station, the rail line passes along the edge of Milltown and Lantyan Woods and then to Woodgate Pill. During the Second World War, the sidings at the pill were used for a munitions store. Next stop was Golant Halt, which served as a passenger station between 1896 and 1965. When the passenger line closed the station was demolished and turned into a car park.

Today the line is leased by the china clay company IMERYS.

With just 110 homes and about 220 residents, the waterside village of Golant has a cosy and picturesque charm.

The village is situated in the parish of St Sampson and the local church bears his name. The life of St Sampson is one of the earliest to be recorded in Cornish history books. The church stands where he settled and made shelter, next to the holy well.

Great food and drink and views across the river can be had from the local pub, the Fishermens Arms.

Golant is a top spot for canoeing, kayaking, sailing and fishing. The Fowey River Canoe Club and Castledore Rowing Club are based here.

Similiar to the Neighbourhood Watch Scheme, residents of Golant are involved in Golant Boat Watch scheme. Their regular river patrols have helped to promote safety and prevent marine crime in the local area.

During the summer months, the Golant Carnival Committee organise a traditional sports and carnival event, which includes everything from sack, egg and spoon and three-legged races to blindfolded kayaking.

Nearby Penpol Creek and Henwood are home to one of the largest heron nesting sites in Cornwall.

When the Friends of the Fowey Estuary carried out the first heronry census in 2013, they counted 12 nest sites and 20 adult herons in the vicinity. In April 2017, they counted 14 occupied nests with 18 herons in the area. Three more nests were recorded at Haye Point.

The first official record of large numbers of herons nesting in the Fowey area was published by the British Birds journal in 1928. The report listed eight breeding pairs at Great Wood, St Winnow. The nesting site has since disappeared but today the British Trust for Ornithology believes the Fowey Estuary has one of the largest heronries in Cornwall.

The grey heron can grow to about 98cms tall and has a wingspan of up to 195cms. Although they prefer a diet of fish, they will also dine out on small birds, ducklings, frogs and rodents.

During Medieval times, merchants from Bodmin anchored at Bodmin Pill to avoid paying landing duties in Lostwithiel. After unloading, goods were carted along small tracks until they reached the main route north, which is today called the Saint's Way.

The sawmills at Bodmin Pill have played an important role in the development of Fowey Docks. In the 1800s the mill produced the timber used to construct the new jetties and during both World Wars the surrounding woodland was coppiced, sawn and sent to the Western Front to make trenches.

In 1974 the sawmills were redeveloped and became home to the first residential recording studio in the UK.

The studio has an international reputation with an impressive list of clients, which includes Oasis, The Verve, Supergrass and Muse.

Fowey Harbour has a long history as a principal trading port of Great Britain providing significant trading links to destinations all over the world.

In 1347 Fowey and Polruan provided 47 ships and 700 men for Royal service to defend Calais, more boats and crew than London.

Commercially, Fowey Harbour is best known as a china clay port and in terms of tonnage, it is the largest clay exporting port in the United Kingdom.

With its close proximity to the china clay producing areas of mid Cornwall and South Devon, china clay or kaolin has been exported through Fowey Harbour for over 150 years.

The first boat to ship china clay from the new jetties in Fowey Harbour was the *Rippling Wave*, built by the Butson family. She set sail in 1869, the same year that Fowey Harbour Commissioners were formed.

The sailing ships of the 1800s could carry 300 tonnes of clay; today the commercial vessels that berth in Fowey routinely load up to 7,500 tonnes.

In 1989, at the peak of modern-day clay mining, a record 1.8 million tonnes of clay were exported from Fowey Docks. Today the port handles 500,000 tonnes per year.

The Cornish nickname for china clay is white gold. As the tin and copper mining industry declined, china clay production increased and diversified Cornwall's mineral trade. Today, the quarries and clay dries operated by IMERYS continue Cornwall's mining history.

Technically speaking kaolin (china clay) is a hydrated aluminium crystalline mineral formed by the hydrothermal decomposition of granite rocks.

Kaolin is represented by the chemical formula $Al_2Si_2O_5(OH)_4$

Geologists believe that the 'kaolinisation' (or the crumbling) came about as a result of two of the earth's processes – hydrothermal (warming) activity and the weather.

The hydrothermal process explains that hot chemical-laden gases rising up from earth into the granite rocks caused them to break into a much softer material.

The weathering process, which came millions of years later, explains that water, which entered the rock through surface cracks, was heated gradually by the radioactive elements in the granite. This warming process slowly decomposed the rock into white clay leaving quartz and mica behind.

The largest use of china clay is in the production of paper.

It's also used as a coating to create the glossy look on magazine covers. It's used to make ceramics, cups, plates and bowls and all manner of bathroom sanitary ware.

And while we're in the bathroom china clay is an ingredient in toothpaste, face powder, face packs and all manner of cosmetics.

China clay is also used to make crayons and create the light diffusing material in white incandescent light bulbs. It's used in paint manufacture, rubber manufacture and in some parts of the world it's used in the production of smoking pipes. In Nepal they use it to whitewash their homes.

In organic farming a light spray of kaolin over certain crops can ward off insect damage and, if you spray it gently throughout an orchard, it stops the sun scalding the fruits' skin. Kaolin is also used to treat an upset stomach and diarrhoea. Some cultures eat it to suppress hunger.

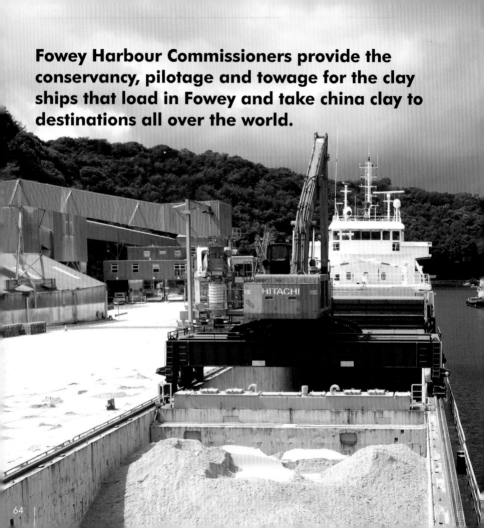

Fowey Harbour Commissioners provide the conservancy, pilotage and towage for the clay ships that load in Fowey and take china clay to destinations all over the world.

Fowey Docks are operated by IMERYS. The cargo, which is brought in either by rail or lorry, is loaded into the ships' holds using an elevator and conveyor belts. The clay ships moor at the custom built New Quay, just beyond Caffa Mill.

The largest ever cargo of clay was in excess of 13,000 tonnes and took 2 days to load. The departure of these heavily laden, deep draught vessels is restricted to high water only. Today over 200 shiploads of clay are exported

Fowey Harbour Commissioners (FHC) has been the chief custodian of the Fowey Estuary since 1869.

FOWEY HARBOUR BOARD OFFICES   FOWEY HARBOUR OFFICES

Since its formation, the Board of Commissioners has been dedicated to protecting the harbour's environment while supporting, facilitating and promoting the many businesses, groups and individuals, whose livelihoods depend upon it.

Set up as a Trust port, all of Fowey Harbour Commissioners' activities are guided by a local group of independent volunteers with a keen interest in the environmental health of the estuary and the economic and social wellbeing of the stakeholders it supports.

Similar to a social enterprise, the Commissioners ensure that any financial surpluses from commercial projects are reinvested straight back into the harbour to benefit all those who operate along and enjoy the river. The estuary has been safeguarded in this way for several generations and the Fowey Harbour Commissioners continue this guardianship today.

The Commissioner's stewardship of the Fowey Estuary begins at Lostwithiel Bridge and ends at the river mouth, between Punches Cross in Polruan and St Catherine's Castle in Fowey.

The Fowey Harbour Office on Albert Quay is the public face of the organisation and under the leadership of the Harbour Master, a team of nearly 30 staff carry out the numerous and varied services the Commissioners provide.

Responsible for an 11km stretch of river that has over 40kms of shoreline, numerous quays, jetties and boatyards, the work of FHC is varied.

Environmentally and socially, the Commissioners work to protect and sustain the habitat and wildlife of the river and maintain the quays, pontoons and moorings so the estuary is safe and accessible for sailors and all kinds of water-sports lovers.

As an open port, the Commissioners have a duty to provide safe haven to any vessel needing to make harbour. As a commercial entity, FHC provides and maintains the navigational aids for the channel as well as the piloting and towage vessels and their skilled personnel.

As chief conductors of all of the waterway traffic, the Harbour Master and his team are the eyes and ears of the river, working night and day to ensure the safe and smooth running of this thriving and much-loved destination.

Fowey Harbour Commissioners operate two tugs whose names are *Cannis* and *Morgawr*.

IMO 8102141

CANNIS

5M
8
6
4

71

The *Cannis* is a Voith tractor tug with a 32-ton bollard pull and the *Morgawr*, another Voith tractor tug, operates a 23.5-ton bollard pull.

Bollard pull, like horsepower in cars, measures the towing or pulling power of a watercraft. The term describes the force exerted by a vessel when it is under full power while attached to a shore-mounted bollard, on a towline.

Fowey Harbour Commissioners coordinate the safe passage of all cargo vessels along the river and are experienced in manoeuvring large ships. They have been operating a towage service since 1881.

The tugs are an essential part of the commercial aspect of Fowey Harbour. They guide vessels to the jetties upstream of the seasonal mooring areas and with inbound ships they can execute a 180-degree turn using up to two tugs per vessel.

Docking at Fowey requires skill. The estuary is narrow and the river twists and bends. Additional fresh water coming down stream creates strong currents that can challenge any captain wanting to berth safely.

For safety reasons all shipping vessels over 37.5 metres have to be escorted into Fowey Harbour by a compulsory pilot. Ships over 95 metres in length need to swing around in the lower harbour using a tug. The tug turns the ship around and pulls it into the loading berth backwards. That way, once loaded the ship can sail straight out.

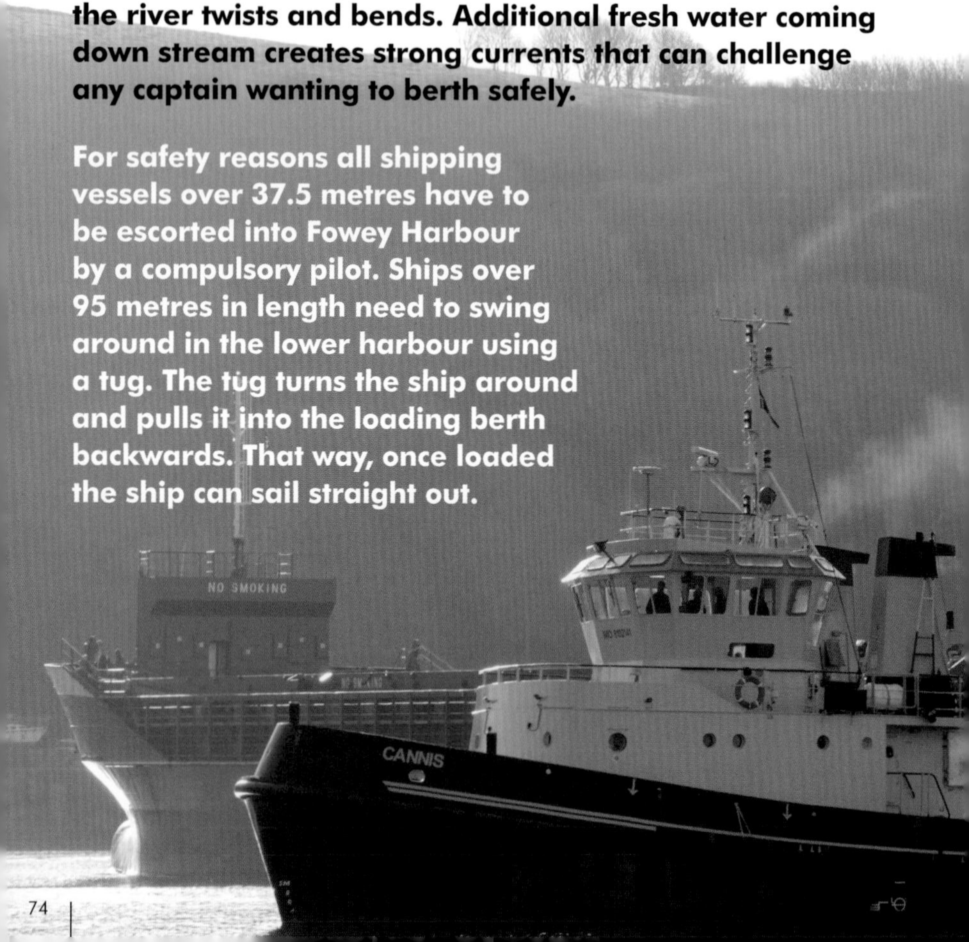

NO SMOKING

CANNIS

Vessels over 120 metres in length have to do the same but with two tugs in operation! The bow tug pulls the ship through the narrows at Caffa Mill into Lew Roads and then it turns through a 90-degree turn into Mixtow Reach.

Fowey Harbour Commissioners provide the pilots and pilot boats essential to all large ships navigating into the Port of Fowey.

Centuries ago, the pilots were rowed out in gigs, a six-oared rowing boat, that competed for business. Today the Fowey pilot is taken to sea in a modern pilot cutter crewed by expert boatmen in whom the pilots entrust their lives to get them aboard ships safely. The pilot cutters are named *Gribbin* and *Gallant*, acknowledging the harbour's landscape and history.

Any large ship requiring entry into Fowey Harbour has to do so under the guidance of a pilot. The Fowey pilots have an extensive local knowledge of the river, its currents and all of the navigational aids. They are also well aware of the ferries and local vessels that regularly make passage across the Fowey river and any special events that might be happening.

As a ship approaches Fowey, it meets the pilot boat at the Pilot station, about 1.5 miles out at sea. Once the pilot boat is safely alongside a rope ladder is lowered and the pilot climbs up into the visiting vessel.

Once safely aboard, the pilot meets the captain and, from the ship's bridge, then conducts the entire navigational process and handles communications, most of which are carried out over VHF radio.

Depending on the needs of the captain, the pilot's duties usually include taking the helm and manoeuvring the ship alongside while coordinating the tugs and liaising with the linesmen, who will secure the ship alongside the jetty.

Pilots are seriously skilled ship handlers, usually former ships captains and master mariners. The Fowey Harbour Commissioners' pilots operate at any time of day or night, often in extreme sea and weather conditions.

Another vital role for Fowey Harbour Commissioners is to maintain the depth of the shipping channel.

With over 430 million litres of water flowing through the channel each day, the shape and level of the seabed is constantly changing.

During the 1900s, silt carried downstream from the mines of Bodmin Moor resulted in a sandbank, which stretched from Penleath Point to Town Quay.

As the china clay industry grew and the number of loading jetties increased, Fowey Harbour Commissioners needed to deepen the harbour so much larger ships could dock and load larger cargos of clay.

In 1922 the Commissioners purchased a steam bucket dredger from the Netherlands for £6,000. Capable of reaching a depth of 13 metres and able to move up to 400 tonnes per hour, the *Tregeagle*, as she was named, was put to work.

Tregeagle served Fowey Harbour Commissioners for over 30 years.

In order to keep the Fowey Estuary navigable for large ships today, the channel is maintained at a depth of six metres below chart datum. That means that vessels drawing up to 8.5 metres can load at all states of the tide.

Maintaining the shipping channel requires constant effort, particularly in the autumn when the trees along the entire estuary shed their leaves into the river. The current carries the leaf litter down stream, where it rots and forms sludge that then sinks to the bottom.

Lantic Bay is named after the beach 1km east of the harbour. She was built by Fowey Harbour Commissioners and their staff, who were determined to create a vessel, in their own boatyard, that would support and sustain the safe and commerical use of the harbour for years to come.

Plans to create a custom-built dredger for Fowey Harbour began on 22nd May 1957. The Harbour Master Captain Mitchell and a team of local seamen, who knew the riverbed and regularly dredged the area, drew up plans for the new vessel. Building works began in July that year at the Commissioners boatyard at Brazen Island and she was launched 12 months later.

At a cost of £60,000 *Lantic Bay* was built by the men of Fowey and Polruan. She started dredging on the 23rd of October 1958 and over six decades later she is still in operation.

As well as supporting the commercial operations of the harbour, the Commissioners are at the heart of Fowey's tourism and leisure industry.

For local boat owners, Fowey harbour is a popular stop over for yachts sailing between Plymouth and Falmouth. Internationally, the harbour welcomes boats from France, Germany, the Netherlands and the USA.

On top of managing 1,500 resident moorings, Fowey Harbour Commissioners welcome 6,000 visiting yachts and motor cruisers each year.

Pont Pill and Mixtow are constantly dredged to support the leisure moorings and the pontoon facilities are constantly updated to meet the needs of overnight and short-stay mariners.

Mixtow is named after the notorious Michelstow or Mixstow family, Mark Mixtow being Fowey's most famous pirate and privateer of the 15th century.

On the southern banks of Mixtow Pill is Penmarlam Quay. Operated by Fowey Harbour Commissioners, Penmarlam provides storage and launching facilities to a wide range of boats. In the winter, this is where local boats are taken out of the water and go to hibernate.

During the summer months, the quay and pontoons are a hive of activity. Local boat owners without a resident mooring are able to store near the quay and launch it as sailing conditions permit.

This sheltered tucked away spot is popular with sailors and watersports enthusiasts of all kinds all year round. After mooring, yachties can grab a shower, order a coffee and even book their engine to be serviced.

Just along the riverbank is Kit's House, which is mentioned in Sir Arthur Quiller-Couch's Cornish romance, *The Astonishing History of Troy Town*. Kit's House was built in 1805 and in the novel it was home to the hero, Mr Fogo. Kenneth Grahame, author of *"Wind in the Willows"* was a frequent visitor.

The Fowey Harbour Patrol Boats that support visiting vessels are named after the characters in the children's television series, *The Magic Roundabout*; Brian, Dylan, Dougal, Ermintrude, Florence and Zebedee.

Bodinnick has been the site of a ferry crossing since at least the 14th century.

In the early days of the Bodinick Ferry, the service was operated under oar.

Trained ferrymen rowed the boats across the river between Bodinnick and Passage Slip in Fowey. The boats could only carry one vehicle at a time. Today, the Bodinnick car ferry is operated by C Toms and Son.

As long as the weather permits, the Bodinnick Ferry service runs every 15 minutes between the slip at Bodinnick and the car park at Caffa Mill. The modern day ferries can carry up to 15 cars, motor homes, minibuses and small lorries.

Bodinnick is believed to get its name from the Cornish word _Bosdinek_, which means "fortified dwelling".

The Old Ferry Inn dates back to the 17th century and would have been an important stop-off when Bodinnick was part of the main southerly route through Cornwall.

On the edge of the Hall Walk, the waterside village is most famous for being the home of the du Maurier family, who bought Ferryside in 1926.

Long before it became a family home, the water's edge plot was a shipyard belonging to John Marks between 1826 and 1846. The yard was then taken over by the Butson brothers and it was there that they built _Rippling Wave_, a 130-ton schooner, which in 1869 was the first ship to carry china clay from the new jetties, just opposite.

Ferryside was originally called Swiss Cottage. As you sail or ferry past today, look out for the _Jane Slade_ figurehead. The room above it is where Daphne du Maurier is believed to have written her first novel, _The Loving Spirit_, inspired by the local Slade family.

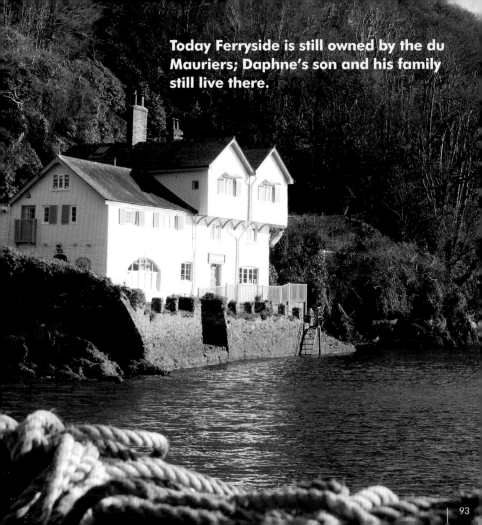

Today Ferryside is still owned by the du Mauriers; Daphne's son and his family still live there.

Daphne du Maurier was born on 13th May 1907. She grew up in London and although her family visited Cornwall during the holidays they didn't buy Ferryside, Bodinnick until 1926.

Du Maurier's first novel *The Loving Spirit*, published in 1931, very fittingly introduced her future husband. Major Tommy Browning was so touched by the book, he made a special voyage to Fowey to meet her. They married in 1932 at Lanteglos Church, just a few miles north of her waterside home.

During the first decade of married life du Maurier only visited Cornwall in the holidays but as war broke out and her husband was called abroad she rented Readymoney Cottage, where she lived with her three children.

Once based in Cornwall she took out a 20-year lease on Menabilly House, which belonged to the Rashleigh family, and moved in 1943. The house, its beaches and the surrounding area were inspiration for a great deal of her writing. In 1969, when the lease expired on Menabilly, she moved to nearby Kilmarth.

Daphne's husband died in 1965 and after living in Cornwall for over 50 years, Dame Daphne du Maurier died in her home in Cornwall on the 19th April 1989. She was cremated and her ashes were scattered on the cliffs near Kilmarth.

Inspired by the novels of Daphne du Maurier and born from an idea to position artwork around Fowey Harbour, Fowey Harbour Commissioners has helped site a sculpture at Berrill's Yard.

Known as the *Rook with a Book* and inspired by du Maurier's 1952 short story *The Birds*, the sculpture was created by Thrussels, a father and son team of metal workers based on Bodmin Moor.

The sculpture was made out of galvanised steel and overlooks the Fowey river and Ferryside, where du Maurier once lived.

Also inspired by local writers and creatives, the Fowey Festival of Arts and Literature takes place in Fowey in May. The week-long event offers a daytime and evening programme of talks, performances and concerts that take place in venues all over the town.

Along the bank from Bodinnick lies a charming little building with a wobbly roof, known as Prime Cellars.

Prime Cellars is one of three old fish cellars that were built between Penleath Point and Wiseman's Stone on the Polruan side of the estuary. Without any vehicular access, the property can only be accessed by boat.

In 1907 Prime Cellars was purchased by Arthur Quiller-Couch (Q) who called it 'the farm'. He rowed across from Fowey almost everyday to look after the land and orchard, which became a popular picnic spot for his family. The house was nicknamed *Priam Cellars*, after the Trojan King.

During the Second World War bombs were dropped on the slopes Q had cultivated and by 1947 the property, which still had its original mud floor, was completely derelict.

In the last few years the house and waterside plot have been carefully and sympathetically restored. As part of the planning requirements, the rebuilding of Prime Cellars had to include maintaining the age-old kink in the roof.

During the 17th and 18th centuries, Fowey thrived on the fishing and processing of pilchards, which were caught in St Austell Bay and exported to the Mediterranean.

Once caught, the pilchards were stored in large cellars, preserved in salt or smoked and then pressed into barrels or hogsheads. The pilchard industry in Fowey peaked in the late 1700s but declined as the price of salt went up and the numbers of shoals went down.

The old fish cellars at Brazen Island and the stretch of woods above were bought by Fowey Harbour Commissioners in 1926. What's left of the buildings are used by the boatyard and the woods are part of the much-loved Hall Walk.

The Hall Walk, which is 6.5km long, is circular and includes two ferry crossings. It can be started in Bodinnick, Fowey or Polruan.

The Hall Walk promenade between Bodinnick to Penleath Point dates back to the 16th century and was created by the Mohun family of nearby Hall Manor. In August 1644, King Charles visited the Mohun family and while strolling the walk he narrowly missed being shot by Parliamentarian troops in Fowey, just opposite.

The Hall Walk wanders through the timeless quayside of Pont, which is only accessible by boat on a high tide.

Despite its remote location, Pont was once a thriving quay, which traded between the farms of the area and other local coastal communities. Grain and logs from the farms were exported in return for coal, flour, manure and stone.

During the 1800s, the tiny settlement was home to a granary, limekilns, and a malt house and sawmill. There was even a pub, which is The Farm House holiday let today. Further down the creek at Pont Pill, there was an isolation hospital. Listed in 1889, it looked after sailors who arrived in the harbour with infectious diseases.

Pont Pill in Cornish is *Pyll Por'Reun*, which means "creek of seal cove".

Built in Polruan in 1870, the *Jane Slade* was a 170-ton fruit schooner that carried oranges from the Azores and pineapples from the West Indies.

Mastered by Thomas Slade, the *Jane Slade* set the record for the fastest passage between the Azores and Bristol. Long before the days of onboard refrigeration, fruit schooners had to be fast so they could deliver their cargo before it was rotten. The schooner was built at Slade's boatyard and Christopher Slade named it after his wife.

During the 19th century, and perhaps owing to their privateering past, the shipbuilders of Fowey and Polruan were renowned for shaping high-speed hulls and schooners. The local boat building industry thrived. The real Jane Slade, who took control of the family shipbuilding business after her husband's death, was the only woman shipbuilder in Cornwall at the time.

Thomas Slade was the inspiration for the character Joseph in Daphne du Maurier's book, *The Loving Spirit*. The *Jane Slade* was also immortalised in the book but renamed the *Janet Coombe*.

Brazen Island gets its name from the island around which it was built, which was first known as Brawn Rock.

Before Brazen Island became part of Fowey's maritime history, the site was originally a quarry, which provided the stone to build property in Fowey and Polruan.

The first boatyard was constructed in 1857 by the Butson family, who were successful shipbuilders from nearby Lanteglos-by-Fowey. In 1881, when the lease to the Butsons expired, Brazen Island became part of Polruan's thriving fishing and pilchard industry. The Brazen Island Sardine Company was incorporated on 25th April 1883 only to liquidate in 1887.

Fowey Harbour Comissioners purchased the land and disused cellars in 1926. During the 1940s the slip was redeveloped by the US Navy and was used by landing craft for the D-Day operations.

Today Fowey Harbour Commissioners operate Brazen Island for the repair and maintenance of their fleet and they also fulfill commercial contracts.

In 2018 Brazen Island was restored to its full capacity. The new slip can handle ships 45 metres in length and the cradle and mobile crane can move and lift vessels weighing up to 500 tonnes.

The boatyards of Brazen Island and Polruan have played an important role in the maritime history of the area.

During the 19th century, Polruan boomed in the shipbuilding industry and at one point was building larger, faster and greater numbers of vessels than Fowey.

Today the largest boatbuilding company still operating along the river is C.Toms and Son. Their boatyard is at the centre of Polruan's boatbuilding history and records suggest the slip has been building ships since 1789.

C. Toms and Son was founded by Charlie Toms in 1922. When Slade's Yard ran into financial difficulty, Charlie, a marine blacksmith, set up his own business and rented Newquay Dock from Fowey Harbour Commissioners.

Having studied marine engineering in Bridport, Charlie's son Jack joined the company and in 1939 they won a contract to carry out repairs for the Admiralty. After the Second World War, the boatbuilding business went into decline so the family began to repair and develop housing.

In the 1950s, C.Toms and Son won a Ministry of Defence (MOD) contract, which put the boat yard back in business. As demand increased for new fishing vessels, a new slipway was built in 1964. Charlie Toms died that year but his grandsons joined the business a year later.

In 1966, Jack Toms was awarded an MBE for his services to the MOD and in 1968 the company bought Slade's Yard. In 1975, they purchased the Bodinnick car ferry and in 1993 they took over the the Polruan Ferry, both of which they still operate today.

In nearly a century of boat building the Polruan based business has gained and maintained a national reputation in the fishing industry and has built vessels for customers all over Great Britain.

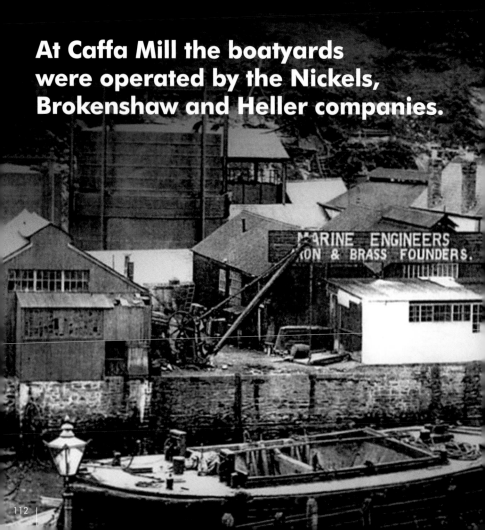

At Caffa Mill the boatyards were operated by the Nickels, Brokenshaw and Heller companies.

MARINE ENGINEERS
IRON & BRASS FOUNDERS.

Joseph Treffry shipped copper from Caffa Mill, before he built the docks at Par. The boat yards closed as the pill silted up but the land was reclaimed and redeveloped during the 1800s by Cornwall's Mineral Railways.

On 20th June 1876 the first passenger service ran between Lostwithiel and Fowey and the railway station opened at Caffa Mill. In 1965 the passenger service was terminated and in 1972, the area was redeveloped into a car park and customs house, which later became the library.

Albert Quay is at the heart of Fowey's maritime leisure industry. The pontoon welcomes thousands of visiting sailors and the adjacent building is the headquarters of Fowey Harbour Commissioners.

Originally known as Broad Slip, Albert Quay was a popular mooring for the fruit schooners of the 1800s. The slipway was renamed Albert Quay in 1846 after a visit from Queen Victoria and Prince Albert. To mark the royal visit a large monument was erected in the centre of the quay, which had to be moved in 1939, to make way for a car park.

When it was moved, the giant granite monument was split into two. The pointed apex was moved to Penleath Point where it was laid in the river and became a landing slip.

The enormous base is now part of the wall surrounding Brazen Island, Fowey Harbour Commissioners' maintenance yard, on the other side of the river.

In 1977, to celebrate Queen Elizabeth II's Silver Jubilee, the pointed apex was reclaimed from the river and re-erected at Caffa Mill.

During medieval times Town Quay was the site of Fowey's Haveners Court, the official office, created by the Duke of Cornwall, for the collection of import and export taxes. It later collected harbour dues.

In 1785 Fowey Town Hall was built encompassing the 15th century guildhall underneath, which was home to the local meat and fish market.

Today the quay is just as busy and colourful. It's the place to book fishing charters and boat trips or you can just sit and enjoy the views across to Polruan.

The Fowey Royal Regatta Week, held in August, is one of Britain's premier sailing events and with plenty of events ashore too, the quay is full of music and laughter. During its long and proud history, the regatta has welcomed royal visitors including Queen Victoria, Prince Albert and Queen Elizabeth II.

Town Quay is also the starting point for the Harbour Swim, which goes from Town Quay to Readymoney Cove and back. The event raises funds for local charities including the RNLI.

The Fowey Royal Regatta is regarded as one of the best local regattas in the country and is designed with families in mind.

Events occur daily on the Town Quay and festivities include a carnival procession, gig racing and spectacular fireworks displays.

All of the regatta events are organised, marshalled and funded by the Fowey Royal Regatta Committee, an entirely voluntary organisation whose members give freely of their time and effort.

The week costs in the region of £30,000 and this money is raised by sponsorship and selling souvenirs, but mainly by street collections – that's an awful lot of pennies in tins!

The most famous festival visitors to Fowey have been the Red Arrows, who first performed at The Fowey Royal Regatta in 1977.

In 2002 the Regatta Committee celebrated the 25th anniversary of the Red Arrows performing in Fowey.

That year determined not to disappoint the crowds, a pilot went through the entire display without any instrumentation – doing the whole show at 400mph entirely from memory.

Crowds from all over Great Britian have flocked to Fowey and Polruan to watch these breath-taking displays. People pack the streets and quaysides and local farmers fill their fields with families.

Regatta week events attract up to 300 visiting boats and over 130 boats from yachts to sailing dinghies, take part in the races.

The first Troy class yachts were built in Fowey in 1929 by Archie Watty.

The boat was designed as a one-off for Sir Charles Hanson, of Fowey Hall, who wanted a boat for his daughter to race competitively. While building the craft, Archie was visited by the local bank manager who was so impressed that he ordered another for himself.

Both boats were racing during the season of 1929 and performed so well that four more locals placed orders. By 1930, six boats of the same design were competing in the harbour. Because of the boat's popularity, the owners created a unique racing class, named *Troy* after the *Troy Town* novels of Sir Arthur Quiller-Couch.

The Troy Class Owners Association was formed and populated by the town's top businessmen, including Sir Charles Hanson, former Lord Mayor of London and Mr Strong, Lloyds bank manager. Dr Moore had Troy no. 3 and Mr Treffry, the local squire, had Troy no. 4. *Amethyst*, Troy no. 5, was built for the local shipbroker, Mr Samuel, and Troy no. 6 was built for the local solicitor, Walter Graham.

In 1970 the last Troy was built in Watty's boatyard; it was number 19 and called *Topaz*. When the yard closed, the Troy Class Owners Association bought the patterns so the building of his boats could continue. Today a total of 29 Troys have been built and 26 of them are still in existence. The last ten have been crafted by John Fuge, Maurice Hunkin, Marcus Lewis, and Peter Williams.

Another distinctive boat unique to Fowey is the Fowey River class dinghy.

The traditional, wooden clinkerbuilt boats have been made in Fowey since the 1950s. Their design was inspired by an article in *Yachting World Magazine*, where readers were encouraged to build their own boats following the plans for a 'knockabout dinghy' created in the 1940s by Reg Freeman.

In the 1950s, Hunkin's boatyard at Polruan built one for the local dentist, others soon followed and by 1957 there were 15 boats in the fleet. By 1965 there were 36.

Left to deteriorate along the shore or on a mooring, the Fowey River dinghy almost disappeared during the 70s and 80s. During the 90s, Hunkin's boatyard began building and restoring some of the old craft and since then Fowey Rivers have had a revival.

Today the racing fleet has up to 25 competitors during Fowey Regatta Week. Look out for these beautiful wooden boats, depicted by their multicoloured sails.

The two racing authorities in Fowey are the Royal Fowey Yacht Club and Fowey Gallants Sailing Club. Both work together as the Port of Fowey Race Organising Committee.

Originally a shipbuilding yard, the history of the Royal Fowey Yacht Club can be traced back to 1894 when it was the Fowey Yacht Club. Permission was granted for the club to use the coronet of the Duke of Cornwall over the shield of the Duchy of Cornwall in 1905 and in 1907 the prefix "Royal" was added to the club's name.

The longest serving commodore was Sir Arthur Quiller-Couch or "Q', his pen name, who remained in office from 1911 until he died in 1944. Q was succeeded by Daphne du Maurier's husband Lt. General Sir Frederick Browning. He became the next commodore and upon retirement in 1962, was elected the club's first admiral.

Lt General Browning was a personal friend of HM The Queen and HRH The Duke of Edinburgh, who visited the club from the Royal Yacht Britannia in July 1962. Today the club has 800 members and its home is a waterside clubhouse.

The Fowey Gallants Sailing Club takes its name from Gallants of Fowey, a group of pirates and privateers operating in Fowey during the 14th and 15th centuries.

Fowey's most successful privateer and pirate was Mark Mixtow. Although Mixtow had a licence to lawfully attack the French, his ships also plundered Flemish, Hanseatic and Spanish vessels. As the stolen goods were sold on in the town, Mixtow's ill-gotten gains grew into a lucrative trade.

Formerly a sail makers, The Fowey Gallants club began in 1947 when Wilfrid Denaro started a water-based youth club teaching local young people how to sail on his yacht *The Gallant*. The club was very popular and in 1972 the Fowey Gallants Sailing Club was formed. Today the club continues to teach children and teenagers to sail. Adult and power boat lessons are available too.

Over the last few decades, Fowey Harbour has become a popular destination for cruise liners. Some of the world's most glamourous ships have anchored in the estuary.

At 43,500 tonnes, the largest cruise ship to enter Fowey Harbour was The World. The luxury liner with 12 decks, 250 crew and 165 residential apartments visited in 2007, 2010 and 2015.

In 2018, and at 227 metres long, the longest cruise ship to anchor in Fowey was the Europa II. With 11 decks, 204 suites and 72m^2 of space for each of its 408 passengers.

There has been a lifeboat operating in the Fowey area for over 150 years. The current station opened at Berrill's Yard in 1997.

The station has two lifeboats, an offshore Trent class *Maurice and Joyce Hardy* and *Olive III*, an inshore D-class vessel.

The station is manned entirely by volunteers and has one paid member of staff, the station mechanic. The crew are on call 24 hours a day, 365 days of the year.

The purpose-built lifeboat station is situated at Berrill's Yard where the Trent class lifeboat is moored on a pontoon. Fowey Harbour Commissioners provide free berthing for the lifeboat with access over the pontoon.

The Polkerris Lifeboat was moved to Town Quay, Fowey in 1922. Lack of horses after the First World War made it more difficult to launch the boat from Polkerris Beach. The old lifeboat station is now *Sam's on the Beach*, a beachside restaurant serving wood fired pizzas.

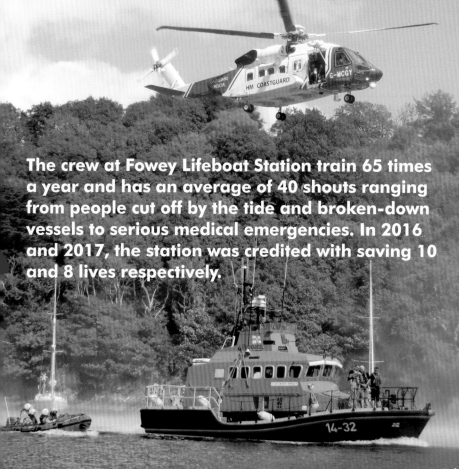

The crew at Fowey Lifeboat Station train 65 times a year and has an average of 40 shouts ranging from people cut off by the tide and broken-down vessels to serious medical emergencies. In 2016 and 2017, the station was credited with saving 10 and 8 lives respectively.

During the 1800s, Cornwall's first lifeboats and rescue craft were rowing boats known as gigs. These 30ft wooden rowing boats, crewed by six rowers, were the early lifeboats and piloted large sailing vessels into local ports.

Today gig rowing is a sport officiated in Cornwall by the Cornish Pilot Gig Association (CPGA), which began in 1986. In just 25 years the sport has developed into an international community of 71 clubs, over 8000 rowers and several hundred boats.

The 200th gig boat was built in Fowey.

Commissioned by the Sidmouth club in Devon, the 32-foot boat was made by Fowey boat builder Louis Hunkin in the family boat yard W.C. Hunkin and Sons.

The Hunkin family have been builders of traditional wooden boats since 1912. The family have built 12 gigs in their time, which are designed along the lines of Treffry, a 32-foot-long pilot gig built in 1838, which the Hunkins have restored.

The River Fowey Gig Club was established in 1988. Their first gig was built by Ralph Bird and named *Rival*, after a vessel that sailed provisions between Plymouth and Fowey. Over the last 20 years, the club has trained competitive teams finishing near the top at the County and World Gig Rowing Championships.

The oldest buildings in Fowey claim
to be Noah's Ark and the Well House,
which were built during the early 1400s.

Built originally as a town house and family home by John Rashleigh in 1570, the oldest pub in Fowey is the Ship Inn. For over four centuries it has been a fireside haven for fishermen, merchants and seafaring travellers.

The King of Prussia pub dates back to the 17th century and is named after the famous pirate and smuggler John Carter, who was "King of Prussia Cove". Since opening in 1765, the King of Prussia has had over 30 landlords.

Today St Austell Brewery leases the building and the land still belongs to the Treffry family of Place. Under the King of Prussia pub was the butter market; a large mural honours the market's history today.

The Russell Inn in Polruan was run by Jane Slade. The pub was named after Prime Minister Lord John Russell. He was the driving force behind the Reform Act of 1832, which introduced significant changes to the electoral system giving more people the right to vote.

The Lugger in Polruan opened as a public house in 1794. Named after a type of Cornish fishing vessel, the pub housed a sail loft, fish cellars and was a private home.

Fowey Aquarium opened beneath the town hall in the oldest part of Fowey in 1952.

Fowey Aquarium is situated on Town Quay and although small in size, it displays an impressive variety of marine creatures. From tiny little goby fish to giant conger eels, most of the fish on display are obtained from local fishermen. Many of its original tanks are still in use.

Everyday at high tide, fresh seawater is pumped into the aquarium, which keeps the filtration of the tanks to a minimum. Although the seawater is sometimes cloudy, the tide flushes in sea squirts, sponges and tube worms that grow on in the aquarium.

In 1931, Fowey Harbour became the record holder for the largest-ever lobster to be caught in European waters.

"Leonard", as he became known, was a dark blue and yellow spotted crustacean that weighed 10kgs and measured over 1.26m from claw to tail.

As well as holding the record for one of Europe's largest ever lobsters, Fowey is also famous for producing particularly large and tasty mussels.

Filter feeding on plankton, mussels are full of fatty acids and minerals such as zinc, iron and folic acid.

Naturally, mussels grow on rocky shores attaching themselves to the rocks by filamentous threads, or beards. Most recently local mussel farmers have developed the industry by growing mussels on ropes in St Austell Bay. Baby mussels floating in the seawater attach to ropes and stay there, feeding on plankton until they reach maturity.

Once fully grown, which can take up to two years, mature mussels are picked and placed in purification tanks, which are fed by the Fowey river. Once cleansed and ready to cook, the mussels are bagged and dispatched to restaurants all over the UK.

Today Fowey mussels are served up in some of the finest restaurants in Great Britain.

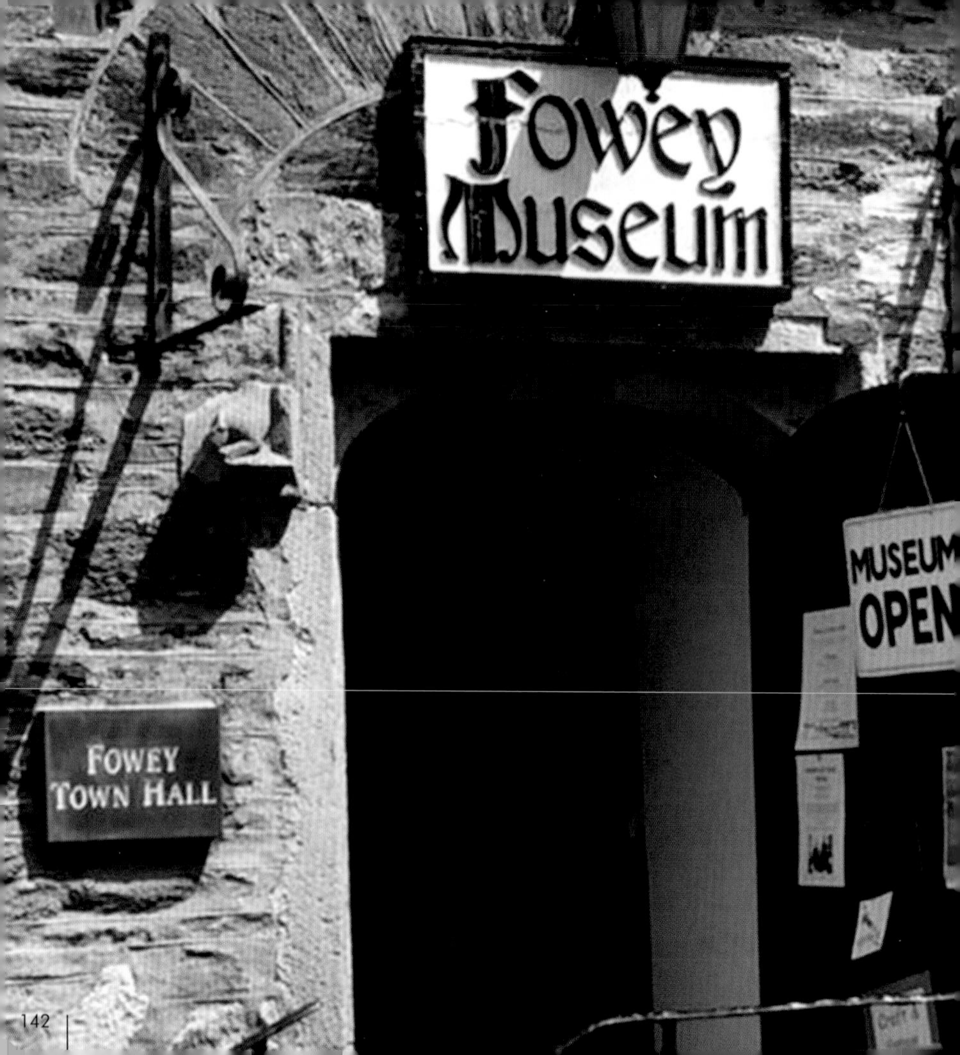
Fowey Museum
FOWEY TOWN HALL
MUSEUM OPEN

The Fowey Museum building dates back to the 1500s and is situated in the heart of the town, opposite the Ship Inn. The lower part was once the town gaol (jail).

The large room occupied by Fowey Museum was once the council chambers. Today it's packed from floor to ceiling with paintings, photographs and ancient documents and exhibits that celebrate Fowey's formidable history.

As well as bringing to life Fowey's extensive maritime past, the displays pay homage to notable visitors and people of the town. The collection also acknowledges the many writers and artists who have been inspired by the natural beauty of the area.

The adjacent Town Hall was built in the 1700s. When Fowey Town Council are not in session, the age-old gathering space is used for weddings, concerts, theatre shows and various community celebrations. It's one of the main venues on the Fowey Festival of Arts and Literature programme.

St Fimbarrus Church in Fowey has the second highest tower in Cornwall. The 36m tower was built during the 1460s from Pentewan stone.

Remains of its Norman past can be seen in the church font but the rest of the building dates back to the 14th and 15th centuries.

The wagon roof is over 500 years old and the 400-year-old pulpit was made from the panelling of a Spanish galleon.

St Fimbarrus is the parish church of Fowey and marks the end of the Saints Way.

The Saints Way, or *Forth An Syns*, is a 43km footpath that bisects Cornwall between the harbours of Padstow on the north coast and Fowey on the south.

The Saints Way begins at the 15th century Church of St Petroc, Padstow and heads south, in part on the Camel Trail, through Little Petherick, St Breock Downs and Lanivet. The path then joins the Fowey river on the edge of Lostwithiel where walkers can take a waterside wander through Golant and then on to Fowey Harbour.

The Saints Way was recovered in 1984 by a group of ramblers who discovered a route of old, forgotten granite stiles near Luxulyan.

The series of ancient paths, which connect chapels and churches and shrines and holy wells, are believed to have been used by the early saints and missionaries as they made their way from Ireland and Wales to Santiago De Compostela in Galicia, Spain.

The route, which is signed with gold and black Celtic cross markers, is also known as the Mariners Way, which would have been first used by Celtic traders as they headed south with tin and gold. Rather than row a risky passage around Land's End, mineral merchants trekked overland, and then sailed from Fowey to Brittany.

Place House has been the home of the Treffry family since the 13th century.

The merchant family became very wealthy during the Middle Ages exporting fish, tin and wool. Today, the family still live there.

In 1457, Fowey was attacked by the French and Place was saved because of the swift action and wits of Elizabeth Treffry. On her suggestion, the house staff stripped the roof of its lead which they boiled and poured over the invaders.

The building was badly damaged and what remains today was developed during the 16th century. The house was remodelled in the 19th century by its famous industrialist resident Joseph Thomas Treffry.

Born in Plymouth in 1782, Joseph Thomas Treffry was a Cornish engineer, industrialist and a miner. Having trained as a civil engineer, Treffry was involved in the construction of the harbours of Newquay and Par and the railway that linked the two.

Between 1839 and 1842, he also developed the Luxulyan viaduct-aqueduct, constructed from granite mined from his own quarries.

The directional light on Whitehouse Quay is affectionately and locally known as the Red Rocket. Its light is visible for 13kms.

Maintained by Fowey Harbour Commissioners, the iconic seven metre tower is an important navigation aid.

It's a sector light, which means the arc of its beam has three colours; white in the middle with red on one side and green on the other. Those sailing into Fowey at night need to stay in the white sector of light. If they start to see red or green, their ship is heading off course.

The Whitehouse area of Fowey was first recorded in 1622 as Whitehouse Meadow. The quay is the main landing place for the Polruan Ferry. On the seaward side, low tide reveals a small sandy beach and children's paddling pool.

The glass and concrete shelter on Whitehouse Quay was presented by the US Navy in recognition of the town's hospitality during the Second World War. Over 1,000 Americans were based in Fowey before they set sail for Normandy in June 1944.

The Whitehouse area of Fowey was once home to Sir Arthur Quiller-Couch (1863 to 1944), who lived at the nearby residence The Haven. Sir Quiller-Couch was one of Fowey's most famous residents.

Sir Arthur Quiller-Couch, who published under the pen name of 'Q', was born in Bodmin in 1863. After achieving a First Class Classics degree at Oxford University he moved to London where he became a journalist. 'Q' first visited Fowey in 1879 and settled at The Haven in 1892.

A prolific writer, penning over 20 novels in his lifetime, Q became Professor of English Literature at Cambridge in 1912, a post he held for the rest of his life.

During his life in Fowey, 'Q' was a very active member of the local community. He played an important role in Cornish society and was made a Bard in 1928.

For many years he was Chairman of Cornwall Education Committee, Chairman of Fowey Harbour Commissioners for more than twenty years, Commodore of the Royal Fowey Yacht Club for more than thirty years and an enthusiastic supporter of liberalism.

Q was knighted in 1910 and was elected Mayor of Fowey in 1937.He died at home in 1944 and he is buried at St Fimbarrus, Fowey Parish Church.

Fowey Hall, which is now a hotel, was built as a family home for Sir Charles Hanson, former Lord Mayor of London, who was born in Fowey in 1846.

Fowey Hall is believed to be one of the inspirations for Toad Hall in Kenneth Grahame's book, *The Wind in the Willows*. Some believe Toad Hall was inspired by Ethy House near Lerryn.

In 1899, Kenneth Grahame first came to Fowey to recover from pneumonia and was introduced to Fowey life by Sir Arthur Quiller- Couch (Q), who became a close friend.

Later that year Kenneth married Elspeth Thomson at Fowey Parish Church and in 1900 their only child Alistair was born. He was blind in one eye and nicknamed Mouse.

The Grahames' marriage was not a happy one so whenever he could, Kenneth escaped to Fowey where he sailed and rowed with his chum 'Q'. It was during these retreats that he began writing to Mouse and his tales from the river became *The Wind in the Willows*.

Fowey Hall was one of the last country houses to be built in England.

Kenneth Grahame penned his son the letters, which would later become books, while he was staying at the Fowey Hotel. Today, original copies of the letters, which were written on headed notepaper, are on display in the hotel.

The Fowey Hotel was designed as a purpose-built hotel in 1882 and constructed for the sum of £5,000. As the Great Western Railway arrived in Cornwall, Fowey's tourist industry grew and the hotel hosted many notable guests, including Kenneth Grahame and Daphne du Maurier.

During World War One the hotel was used as a convalescent home for wounded soldiers and in World War Two, it was taken over by the British Government and housed US naval officers until 1945.

Today, the classic Victorian hotel has retained many original features, including a working period lift. The lower garden area just across the Esplanade, which is right by the water's edge, is a top spot to try a traditional Cornish cream tea.

Point Neptune is a 40-room villa built in 1862 for local landowner William Rashleigh. The stunning Italianate mansion was built on the site of a Napoleonic gun battery, once part of Fowey's harbour defences. Only the remains of the buttresses can be seen today.

Daphne du Maurier lived in the coach house, now Readymoney Cottage, during the Second World War where she wrote her 1942 novel, *Frenchman's Creek*.

In the early 19ᵗʰ century, Readymoney Cove was known as 'Porth Mundy', which means 'mineral house'. Today it's a popular beach for families.

During the 1800s, the cove was an important part of the local pilchard industry. In 1792, and on the site of an old gun emplacement, giant pilchard cellars were built. The cellars were 16m long, 24m wide and had walls over 60cms thick. The buildings housed and processed the fish caught in St Austell Bay before they were packed into hogsheads and shipped.

A hogshead was a wooden cask that could hold over 52 litres. At that time and in one year alone, over 60,000 hogsheads of pilchards could be exported from Fowey - that's about 14 million litres of fish - the same volume as six olympic swimming pools.

St Catherine's Castle was built by Thomas Treffry of Place in 1542. It was constructed as part of Henry VIII's chain of harbour defences, which ran along the English Channel coast.

The D-shaped fort was constructed with extensive views of the harbour mouth, to supplement the blockhouses already positioned opposite one another at Fowey and Polruan.

Gunports were situated on the ground and first floors and a parapet walkway had high battlements either side. During the Crimean War in 1855, the bastion was updated with a battery for two guns and an ammunition store, which was built into the rocks.

During the Second World War a concrete shelter and pill box were added. The fort then became an observation post and detonation point for a controlled minefield, which was laid across the river mouth to protect from German invasion. Today English Heritage manages the castle, admission is free and the site is open all year.

Maintained by Fowey Harbour Commissioners, St Catherine's light was built in 1908. Its light covers the hazardous waters of the Cannis rock and the eastern shore.

The bold red lighthouse is built on the site of St Catherine's chapel. During medieval times, the chapel kept a light burning as a way to signal dangerous waters and landfall to ships.

The earliest surviving maritime defences of Fowey Harbour known as the Blockhouses were built during Medieval times.

The four storey towers were constructed with walls 2m thick to defend the harbour against foreign invasion.

Positioned on the banks at Fowey and Polruan, the rectangular towers were linked by a chain, 40cms thick, which could be raised across the harbour entrance in event of an attack.

In 1474 the chain was removed under the orders of King Edward IV. It was given to the 'Men of Dartmouth' as a way to punish the Fowey privateers who were still attacking French ships, despite a peace treaty between France and the English Crown.

Built at the foot of a very steep hill, Polruan is surrounded on three sides by water; Pont Creek to the north, the English Channel to the south and the River Fowey to the west.

The sheltered waters of Polruan Pool have made it a safe haven for boats and boatbuilders for centuries.

Polruan is named after St Ruan, who settled on the site that is now the ruin of St Saviour's Church. The word Polruan in Cornish is *Porthruwan*, which means the harbour (porth) of a man called Ruwan.

Situated 73 metres up on the top of St Saviour's Hill, the Polruan National Coastwatch Institution (NCI) station overlooks a sea area from Lizard Point to the west to the Eddystone Lighthouse in the east.

The Polruan station is manned entirely by local volunteers. Their job as watch keepers is to keep an eye on the local coastline and raise the alarm should they see anyone or any vessel in difficulty. As long as they're not engaged in an incident, the watch keepers at Polruan welcome visitors to the lookout.

There are 50 NCI stations along the British coastline manned by over 2,000 volunteers. NCI watch keepers are the eyes and ears of the coast and play an important role in the preservation and protection of life at sea.

The solitary white cross on the eastern side of the entrance to Fowey Harbour is known as Punches Cross.

While local historians believe the cross marked the limit of the authority of the Prior of Tywardreath, legend has it that it was the landing place of the boy Jesus, who travelled to Fowey with his uncle, Joseph of Arimathea.

The origin of the name Punches Cross is also a bit of a mystery. One story says it's derived from Pont's Cross, named after the monk who collected the harbour taxes and lived in Pont. Another suggests it is named after Pontious Pilate, who also landed in Fowey. Whatever its history, the cross has been an inspiring landmark at the entrance to Fowey symbolising good over evil.

Today it is an important navigation mark at the mouth of the estuary and is looked after by Fowey Harbour Commissioners.

To the west of Fowey, the two beautiful but slightly haunting beaches at Polridmouth are part of the Menabilly Estate.

Menabilly House has been the seat of the Rashleigh family since the 16th century. Today the Georgian-style mansion house is a Grade II listed building and still occupied by the family.

During the late 1800s and with an estate of over 30,156 acres, about 4% of Cornwall's landmass, Jonathan Rashleigh was the largest landowner in Cornwall.

The ornamental lake at Polridmouth beach was used as a decoy for Fowey Harbour during the Second World War. Lights were positioned around the edge of the water to lure air assaults away from the real harbour.

At low tide, on the westerly beach, it's possible to see what remains of the wreck of the *Romaine*. On 16th January 1930, as she made her way in ballast between Par and Fowey she was caught in a sudden storm. The ship lost power and was tossed onto the rocks on the beach. Her captain and crew made it ashore and the decision was made not to salvage her.

Most famously Menabilly House and Polridmouth Beach are believed to be the inspirational settings of Manderley in Daphne du Maurier's novel _Rebecca_.

For any vessel wanting to make safe harbour into Fowey, or the shallower ports in St Austell Bay, the Daymark at Gribbin Head has been an important navigational point since its construction in 1832.

William Rashleigh of Menabilly, who granted the land for the tower, requested they 'make the Beacon an ornament to my grounds'; thus the tenders issued by Trinity House were for a 'very handsome Greco Gothic Square Tower'.

The National Trust acquired the land around Gribbin Head in 1967. They open the tower every Sunday from July to early September.

The Daymark is 26 metres tall, with 109 steps to the top. It has never been illuminated – instead its outstanding red and white bands ensure it can be seen during the day. It's been a Grade II listed building since 1974.

Although almost impossible to imagine, there was once a time, just a few centuries ago, when the motor car and tarmac for roads had not been invented. Everything was made, mined, moved and ploughed by muscle and the fruits of those labours were either transported by horses or under sail.

Little more than 150 years ago, the Fowey river would have been the dual carriage way of the area and the motorways were the English Channel and Atlantic Ocean. In the same way that the Thames was "liquid gold" for London, carrying riches in and out of the capital, the Fowey River was the lifeblood of South East Cornwall.

It's humbling to consider that just a few generations ago, the livelihoods of the rich and the poor depended entirely upon on the ebb and flow of the Fowey river and its links to the sea. Cornwall's awesome mineral trade could not have developed industrial Europe without its resourceful landlubbers and their friends and colleagues, who sailed the high seas.

It's no surprise that during Cornwall's mining heyday, and centuries before, The Crown, local land owners and influential stakeholders organised themselves as Trusts, to safeguard the county's ports and harbours.

Whilst the Fowey Estuary no longer needs canons or chains to defend its riches and activities, livelihoods and the health of the river itself still require guardianship.

Compared to the past, 21st century lives are time poor and resource hungry and the ability for goods to be transported by sea is as important today as it ever was. Modern ships are able to carry vast amounts of cargo, even the comparatively small ships which pass through Fowey carry about 3000 tonnes of china clay. For each shipload that's 120 lorries off our roads.

Fowey Harbour is still a significant port for Great Britain but more and more this exquisite part of Cornwall is becoming a tourist centre and holiday destination for those needing a break from the modern world. Today, the towns and villages along the River Fowey have become much-loved retreats, weekend breakaways or a regular holiday spots for individuals, couples and families who want to enjoy this beautiful part of Cornwall.

But the timelessness and unspoilt beauty of the Fowey Estuary today is no accident. Through their careful management, Fowey Harbour Commissioners have protected and promoted commercial activities on the river, but also preserved the creeks and quays, wildlife and landscape. Today 150 years on, that guardianship continues apace so that this inspiring and rich river estuary can be enjoyed by generations to come.

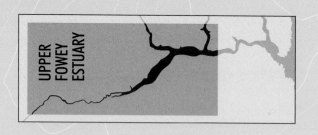

UPPER FOWEY ESTUARY

← GOLITHA FALLS
RESPRYN
LANHYDROCK HOUSE

LOSTWITHIEL

Shirehall Moor Salt Marsh

Woodgate Pill ■

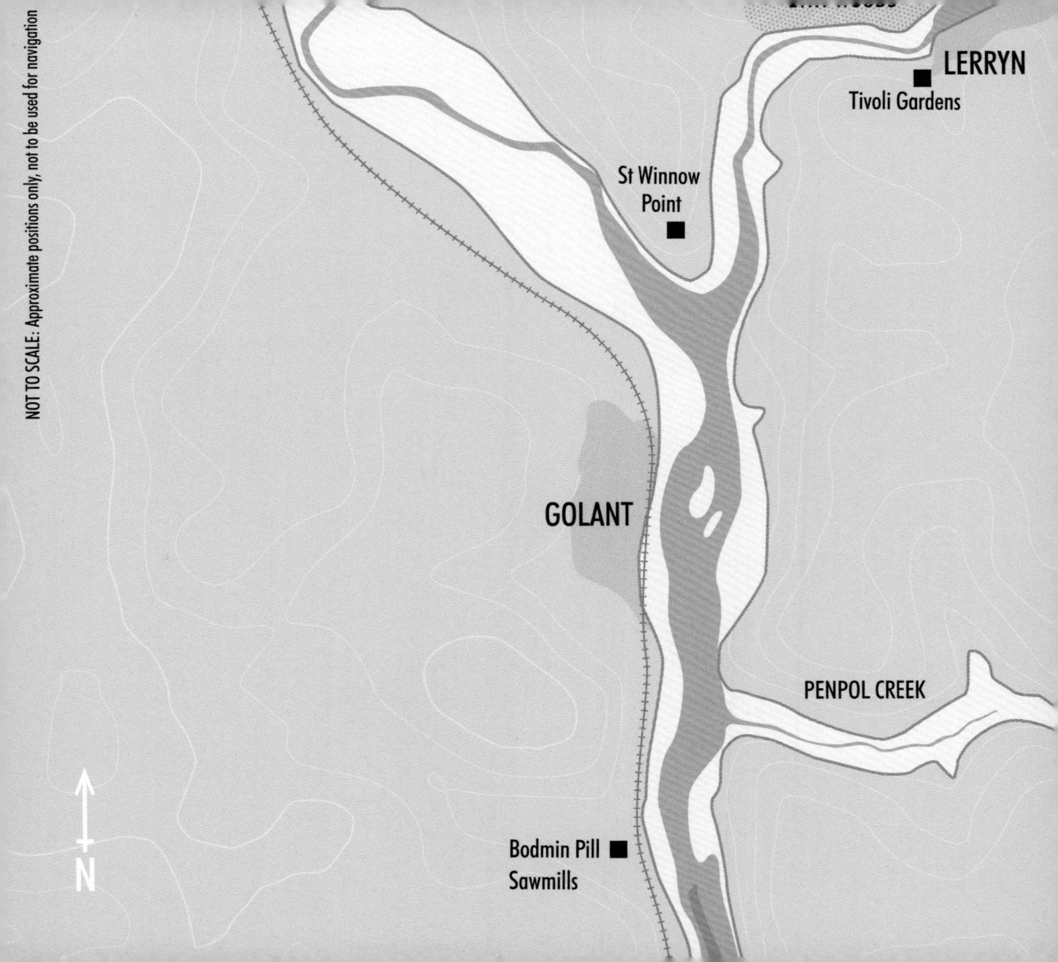
LERRYN
Tivoli Gardens
St Winnow
Point
GOLANT
PENPOL CREEK
Bodmin Pill
Sawmills
N
NOT TO SCALE: Approximate positions only, not to be used for navigation

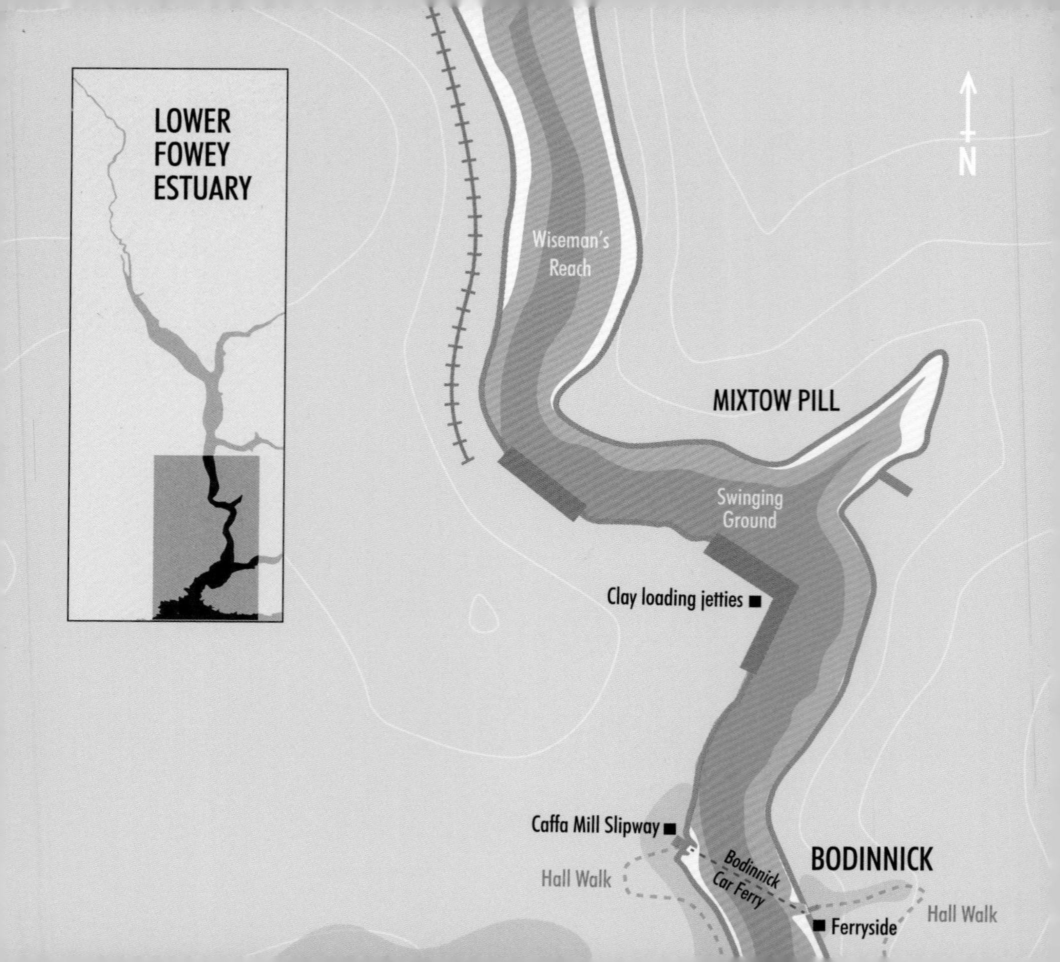

LOWER FOWEY ESTUARY

MIXTOW PILL

Swinging Ground

Wiseman's Reach

Clay loading jetties

Caffa Mill Slipway

Bodinnick Car Ferry

BODINNICK

Ferryside

Hall Walk

Hall Walk

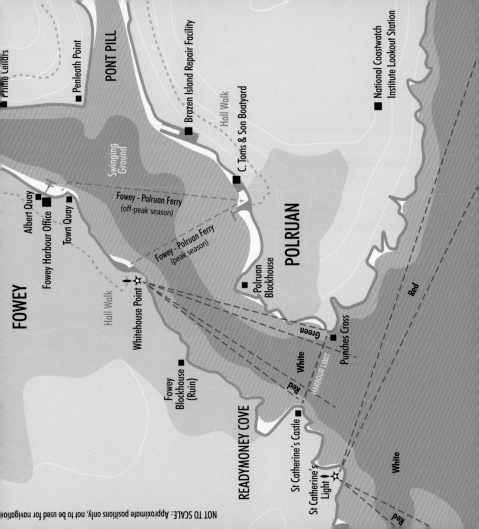

FOWEY

POLRUAN

PONT PILL

READYMONEY COVE

Prime Cellars
Penleath Point
Brazen Island Repair Facility
Hall Walk
C. Toms & Son Boatyard
National Coastwatch Institue Lookout Station
Swinging Ground
Albert Quay
Fowey Harbour Office
Town Quay
Fowey - Polruan Ferry (off-peak season)
Fowey - Polruan Ferry (peak season)
Polruan Blockhouse
Whitehouse Point
Hall Walk
Fowey Blockhouse (Ruin)
Green
Punches Cross
White
HARBOUR LIMIT
Red
Red
St Catherine's Castle
White
St Catherine's Light
Red

Thank you to Paul Colledge, Marcus Lewis, Lostwithiel Business Group, Shutterstock and Fowey Harbour Commissioners for access to their photographic collections. Photo credits as follows:

Cover	David Jenner
Page 20	Lostwithiel Bridge copyright The Francis Frith Collection
Page 30	Kingfisher, copyright Ian McCarthy
Page 46	Copyright Keith Jenkin Cornwall Railway Society
Page 48	Golant, copyright The Francis Frith Collection
Page 50	Alamy
Page 53	Wading Heron, copyright Encounter Cornwall
Page 54	The Noah's Ark Archive
Page 60	IMERYS History Society
Page 62	David Jenner
Page 94	Alamy
Page 100	The Noah's Ark Archive
Page 103	Pont Pill copyright The Francis Frith Collection
Page 110	C.Toms and Sons
Page 130	Europa, Joe Tomlin
Page 136	The Noah's Ark Archive
Page 144	St Fimbarrus copyright The Francis Frith Collection
Page 148	Place House copyright The Francis Frith Collection
Page 155	Fowey Hall Hotel
Page 157	Fowey Hotel
Page 166	David Jenner

Additional thanks to:

Nick Gill, Claire Hoddinott, Alex Lewis, Marcus Lewis and Paul Thomas

Fowey Harbour Heritage Society - www.foweyharbourheritage.org.uk

Fowey Museum

Lerryn Historical Society - www.lerrynhistory.co.uk

Lostwithiel Museum

Mike Sutherland - www.foweyharbourhistory.com

References and Bibliography

Fowey Estuary Historical Audit, Catherine Parkes, (Cornwall Archaeological Unit; 2000)

Fowey, A Brief History, Kerdroya / Ivor Spreadbury BA (Fowey Museum Trust; 2004)

Cornish Place Names and Language, Craig Weatherhill (Sigma Leisure; 2007)

Rediscover Fowey, Paul Richards (Palace Printers; 1996)

Exploring the Fowey Valley, Paul Lightfoot (Alison Hodge; 2011)

Visitors Guide to the Fowey Estuary, Liz Luck (Cornwall County Council; 2000)

The New Book of Lostwithiel, Barbara Fraser (Halsgrove; 2012)

The Environment Agency - www.gov.uk

The National Trust - www.nationaltrust.org.uk

Westcountry Rivers Trust - www.wrt.org.uk

Friends of Fowey Estuary - www.friendsofthefowey.org.uk